THE IMPACT OF ENVIRONMENTALISM:
THE LANDSCAPE

Neil Morris

www.raintreepublishers.co.uk
Visit our website to find out more information about Raintree books.

To order:
☎ Phone 0845 6044371
🖷 Fax +44 (0) 1865 312263
🖳 Email myorders@raintreepublishers.co.uk

Customers from outside the UK please telephone +44 1865 312262

Raintree is an imprint of Capstone Global Library Limited, a company incorporated in England and Wales having its registered office at 7 Pilgrim Street, London, EC4V 6LB – Registered company number: 6695582

Edited by Andrew Farrow, Adam Miller, and Diyan Leake
Designed by Victoria Allen
Picture research by Elizabeth Alexander
Illustrations by Oxford Designers & Illustrators
Originated by Capstone Global Library Ltd
Printed and bound in China by Leo Paper Products Ltd

ISBN 978 1 406 23860 0 (hardback)
16 15 14 13 12
10 9 8 7 6 5 4 3 2 1

British Library Cataloguing in Publication Data
A full catalogue record for this book is available from the British Library.

Acknowledgements
The author and publisher are grateful to the following for permission to reproduce copyright material: Alamy pp. 25 top (© Richard Levine), 38 (© Imagebroker), 40 (© Robert Harding Travel/Tony Waltham), 45 (© Alaskastock), 50 (© John Henshall), 55 (© Hemis/ Guiziou Franck); Corbis pp. 10 (© Geoffrey Clements), 13 (© Reuters/Daniel Aguilar), 22 (© Russ Heinl), 48 (© Du Huaju/XinHua/Xinhua Press); Image created by James Corner Field Operations. Use courtesy of the City of New York p. 25 bottom; Getty Images pp. 33 (AFP/Amy Coopes), 43 (Scott Olson); Mr Giacomo Nicolini, KeitaLAB, IBIMET-CNR, 2007 p. 36; Photolibrary pp. 15 top and bottom (Still Pictures/Bruce Molnia/ USGS), 26 (age fotostock/Alan Kearney); Shutterstock pp. 6 (© Mariusz S. Jurgielewicz), 9 (© mambo6435), 16 (© Euro Color Creative), 19 (© L. Barnwell), 47 (© Krzysztof Wiktor), 52 (© BlueOrange Studio), 56 (© BESTWEB); © Wismut GmbH p. 21 top and bottom; www.unep.org/wed p. 28.

Cover photograph of (top) a coal-fired power station, reproduced with permission of Shutterstock (© Danicek), and (bottom) a wind turbine, reproduced with permission of Shutterstock (© Martin D. Vonka).

Every effort has been made to contact copyright holders of material reproduced in this book. Any omissions will be rectified in subsequent printings if notice is given to the publisher.

CONTENTS

Words printed in **bold** are explained in the glossary.

ENVIRONMENTAL REVOLUTION

Environmentalists are people who want to look after their natural surroundings. They care about the environment, which includes all the Earth's land and sea, as well as the air that we need to breathe. Taking such care might seem an obvious thing to do, and most of us try hard not to spoil or harm our surroundings. But however hard we try, there are always problems to overcome.

We all produce rubbish every day. We all use our share of precious resources, such as water. We use cars and buses that give off harmful exhaust gases. The factories that make our clothes and computers take up space and cause pollution. Environmentalists are concerned about all these issues, and many more. But what impact have their thinking and their decisions had on our landscape? In this book we shall find out.

What is the "landscape"?

When environmentalists talk about the landscape, they mean the natural scenery around them. Geographers often call different kinds of scenery "physical features" or "landforms". The landscape is made up of features such as mountains, valleys, and plains. The Earth's landforms also include lakes and rivers. There are seascapes as well as landscapes, including bays, peninsulas, and coasts. And there are the world's cityscapes that are full of urban scenery. All these features concern environmentalists.

All over the world

The Earth's physical features vary around the world. The hot, wet rainforests of South America, Africa, and south-east Asia, for example, are very different from the colder forests of North America and northern Europe and Asia. But environmentalists care about all the world's forests and try to have an impact on everyone's attitude towards them. The same is true of all other landscapes. In this book, we look at examples from all over the world, as the map opposite shows. Environmentalism, meaning the protection of the natural environment, started as a small movement. It now reaches across the globe.

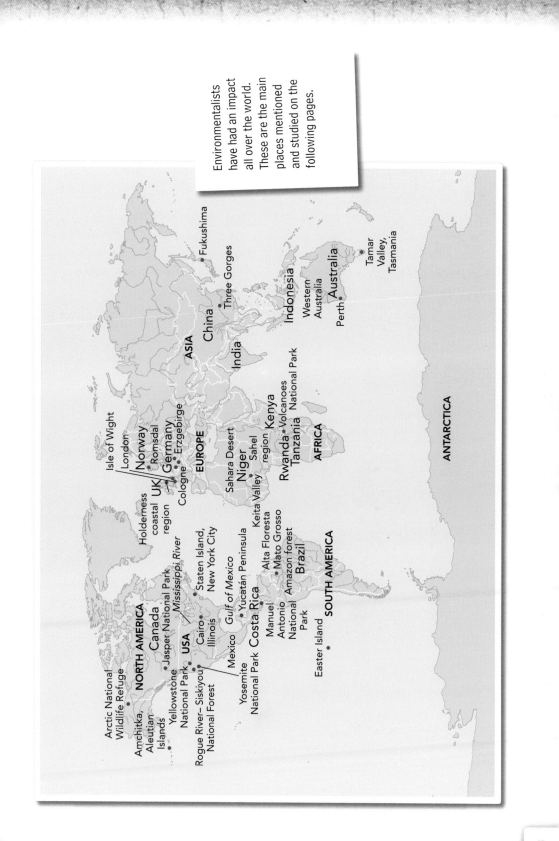

Environmentalists have had an impact all over the world. These are the main places mentioned and studied on the following pages.

NORTH AMERICA

Arctic National Wildlife Refuge
Amchitka, Aleutian Islands
Canada
Jasper National Park
Yellowstone National Park
Rogue River–Siskiyou National Forest
Yosemite National Park
USA
Cairo, Illinois
Staten Island, New York City
Mississippi River
Holderness coastal region
Gulf of Mexico
Mexico
Yucatán Peninsula
Costa Rica
Manuel Antonio National Park

SOUTH AMERICA

Easter Island
Amazon forest
Alta Floresta
Mato Grosso
Brazil

EUROPE

Isle of Wight
London
UK
Norway
Romsdal
Germany
Cologne
Erzgebirge

AFRICA

Sahara Desert
Niger
Keita Valley
Sahel region
Rwanda
Tanzania
Kenya
Volcanoes National Park

ASIA

China
Three Gorges
Fukushima
India
Indonesia

AUSTRALIA

Western Australia
Perth
Tamar Valley, Tasmania
Australia

ANTARCTICA

7

Changing attitudes

Early environmentalists, such as John Muir (see panel, opposite), were interested in keeping wilderness areas in their natural state. In 1901, Muir wrote: "None of Nature's landscapes are ugly so long as they are wild." Many early environmentalists shared this belief. They saw the landscape as something beautiful and unspoiled. It was often made up of dramatic mountain peaks, scenic lakes, and fast-running streams and rivers.

However, attitudes changed during the 20th century, as towns and cities grew larger. People still wanted to keep "wild nature", and at the same time they became interested in less picturesque landscapes. Environmentalists turned their attention to protecting people's everyday surroundings from the effects of pollution. These surroundings included towns and villages, as well as the countryside and coasts.

The Sierra Nevada mountain range in California, USA, is the type of landscape that early environmentalists such as John Muir wanted to protect. Muir himself spent a great deal of time in these beautiful mountains.

A "wild" vs "useful" landscape

In 1903, the city of San Francisco, USA, suggested building a dam in the Hetch Hetchy Valley within Yosemite National Park. John Muir called the valley a "holy temple" and was bitterly opposed to the dam, which was intended to provide water for the city. Many people felt that this was an important use of a valley and a river, and it was completed in 1923. Some local environmentalists are still opposed to it.

Then and Now
Founder of the Sierra Club

John Muir (1838–1914) was a Scottish-born American naturalist and wilderness explorer. His family moved to the United States when he was 11. After studying in Wisconsin, Muir hiked across the country to California. He wrote studies of the Yosemite Valley and urged politicians to turn it into a national park. He even camped there with US President Theodore Roosevelt, and his wish was granted in 1890. Two years later Muir founded an environmental organization and named it after a Californian mountain range. Today the famous Sierra Club has more than 1.3 million members. One of the Club's aims is "to educate and enlist humanity to protect and restore the quality of the natural and human environment".

Changing jobs

As attitudes have changed towards the landscape, environmentalism has had a different, greater impact. One of its many favourable effects has been to create all sorts of new jobs. In the US National Park Service, for example, there are opportunities for young people to start many different careers. The Service advertises jobs for:

- administrators
- archaeologists
- architects
- community planners
- engineers
- financial managers
- firefighters
- health and safety officers
- historians
- human resources staff
- landscape architects
- park police
- park rangers.

Going green

Since the early 1970s, the word *green* has been used to mean "environmental" or "environmentally friendly". *Green* comes originally from *grass* and *grow*, so it made sense to link the colour with the natural world. In 1971, a small group of activists decided to call themselves Greenpeace. Forty years later, this has become an enormous organization, and it still uses the same name. It was not long before there were Green Parties trying to win votes in political elections, first in New Zealand, Germany, and Belgium, and then in the UK and USA. By 2001, there was even a worldwide network of environmental political movements, called the Global Greens.

INDUSTRIALIZED WORLD

Who were the first environmentalists, and what impact did they have on their landscape? Historians might argue that people of ancient civilizations had the first ideas about conservation, which means preserving, protecting, and managing the natural environment. For example, the ancient Phoenicians of south-west Asia made flat **terraces** on hillsides more than 3,000 years ago. They wanted to use rainwater more wisely in order to stop soil erosion and to help crops grow. The ancient Chinese used similar methods, and hillside terracing is still used all over the world today.

Ancient ideas

The ancient Greeks realized that some farming techniques were bad for the land. They introduced the practice of **rotating** crops. Some of their greatest thinkers put their minds to what we today call environmentalism. Writing in the 4th century BC, the **philosopher** Plato described how forests were being cut down to provide wood for the houses and ships of Athens.

> "But at that epoch [time] the country was unimpaired, and for its mountains it had high arable hills, and … it had much forest land in its mountains, of which there are visible signs even to this day; for there are some mountains which now have nothing but food for bees, but they had trees no very long time ago."
>
> Plato

From agriculture to industry

It is difficult to know how much of an impact ancient thinkers' ideas had on farmers, politicians, and the environment. We know more about those who wanted to protect the landscape in more recent times. In the late 18th and early 19th centuries, all sorts of people, from philosophers to poets, saw dangers in the rise of industry.

The **Industrial Revolution**, as we call it now, began in Britain and spread to the rest of Europe and the United States. Factories opened, using new kinds of machinery. They were mainly powered by steam, which was produced by burning coal. As Britain had large deposits of coal, it swiftly changed from an agricultural to an industrial society.

Getting coal meant sinking mines, and these altered the landscape with their deep holes, industrial buildings, and piles of waste. Towns and cities sprawled out into the countryside as people moved to find work. Labourers built canals, railways, and roads to carry coal and goods. All these industrial developments had an impact on the landscape.

The remains of early industrial development, like this Cornish tin mine, can still be seen in the UK's landscape.

William Morris

The effects of the Industrial Revolution led many 19th-century writers and artists to question its impact on the landscape. One of the most influential was William Morris (1834–1896), who practised traditional methods of textile production, printing, and other craftwork. He believed that the beauty of the British countryside was threatened by industrial pollution. In 1884, Morris wrote:

"No one for instance [is] to be allowed to cut down, for mere profit, trees whose loss would spoil a landscape: neither on any pretext should people be allowed to darken the daylight with smoke, to befoul rivers, or to **degrade** any spot of earth with squalid litter and brutal wasteful disorder."

ENVIRONMENTALISM IN ACTION

World's first national park

One of the early environmentalists' great achievements was the establishment of protected areas. Their reaction to the destruction of the landscape led politicians to think about how to conserve areas of natural beauty. This came about first in the United States, where the world's first national park opened in 1872. This was Yellowstone National Park, which covers the north-western corner of the state of Wyoming, with parts extending into the states of Idaho and Montana.

The beginnings

During the 1830s, an explorer and trapper named Jim Bridger (1804–1881) ventured into the wilderness surrounding the canyon of the Yellowstone River. Bridger came out with extraordinary tales of boiling springs, giant **geysers**, and spectacular waterfalls. He said he had even seen petrified trees (trees turned to stone), which many people found difficult to believe. But all his stories turned out to be true (the petrified trees were buried by volcanic eruptions 45–50 million years ago). By the late 1860s, mining prospectors and hunters were visiting the area, which led others to worry about preserving this amazing landscape.

This painting, which shows the Grand Canyon in Yellowstone Park, was painted in 1872 by Thomas Moran.

Creating the park

In 1871, a **geologist** named Ferdinand Hayden (1829–1887) led a horseback expedition of 37 men to make a survey of the Yellowstone region. They too were amazed by what they saw, and Hayden wrote a 500-page report. This, along with paintings and photographs, convinced the doubters. On 1 March 1872, US President Ulysses S. Grant officially created Yellowstone National Park. Nearly 9,000 square kilometres (3,475 square miles) of wilderness became "a public park or pleasuring ground for the benefit and enjoyment of the people".

Tourist attraction

Today Yellowstone has nine visitor centres, 12 campgrounds, and more than 2,000 campsites, as well as hotels, cabins, general stores, and gift shops. There are guided tours and a wide range of activities, including backpacking, boating, cycling, fishing, hiking, horse-riding, and watching wildlife.

National Park Service

In 1916, the US government set up a service to oversee the nation's 37 protected areas. Today there are 58 national parks and a further 336 protected areas. They cover an area of more than 340,000 square kilometres (131,000 square miles). That is an area nearly the size of Germany. The largest is Wrangell-St. Elias National Park and Preserve in Alaska, established in 1980, which is more than five times bigger than Yellowstone. The National Park Service employs about 22,000 professional staff and has 221,000 volunteers.

Visitor numbers

The numbers of visitors to Yellowstone National Park have risen throughout its history. More than 152 million people have visited the park since it opened.

Year	Number of visitors
1872	300
1880	1,000
1890	7,808
1900	8,928
1910	19,575
1920	79,777
1930	227,901
1940	526,437
1950	1,109,926
1960	1,443,288
1970	2,297,290
1980	2,000,273
1990	2,823,572
2000	2,838,233
2010	3,640,904

Direct action

Many environmental groups sprang up during the 20th century. They take different approaches to green issues. Some try to influence politicians, decision-makers, and the general public by making them aware of problems. Others take more direct action, especially by trying to stop things happening that they think are wrong.

The best-known direct-action group is Greenpeace, which calls itself "a campaigning organization which uses non-violent, creative confrontation to expose global environmental problems, and to force the solutions which are essential to a green and peaceful future".

Greenpeace was founded in 1971 to protest against the testing of nuclear weapons in Alaska. The founders felt the tests would pollute the Alaskan landscape, endangering many animals and possibly setting off earthquakes. They believed that a few individuals could make a real difference.

The nuclear test still went ahead, but the protesters gained a lot of publicity and support around the world. Thirty years later, scientists were still concerned that radiation from the blast might have leaked into the sea and could be harming marine animals and plants.

The growth of Greenpeace

Members of Greenpeace became known as "eco-warriors", a term for activists who take direct action on environmental issues. Since the early 1970s, Greenpeace International has widened its campaigns to cover many issues and now has offices in 41 countries and 2.9 million members. Today, its campaigns focus on six main topics:

- climate change (how to combat it)
- forests (saving them)
- oceans (keeping them clean)
- agriculture (producing healthy food)
- pollution (stopping it ruining our land, sea, and air)
- nuclear power (stopping its use).

The campaign to combat climate change (see page 14) is very important. Greenpeace says that **global warming** is a severe threat to many natural landscapes. These include glaciers, coral reefs, forests, wetlands, and grasslands.

Greenpeace activists laid out this SOS banner in a forest in Mexico. The distress signal is meant to show that instead of being protected, the forest is being stripped of its trees.

Friends of the Earth

Friends of the Earth (FoE) calls itself a "grassroots environmental network". It has 76 national member groups, about 5,000 local activist groups around the world, and more than 2 million members and supporters. FoE was founded in 1969 by David Brower (1912–2000), a former director of the Sierra Club (see page 7). Brower has been called the greatest environmentalist of the 20th century, and his most famous saying was: "We do not inherit the Earth from our fathers, we are borrowing it from our children." FoE tries to use persuasion towards change rather than direct action, and has shown that this can be a very effective form of environmentalism.

Arne Naess

The Norwegian philosopher and mountaineer Arne Naess (1912–2009) was a man of action, an eco-warrior, and a great thinker. In 1950, he led the first expedition to conquer the 7,708-metre (25,289-foot) Tirich Mir Mountain in Pakistan. Twenty years later, he chained himself to rocks in front of a waterfall in Norway, and refused to move until plans to build a **hydroelectric plant** were dropped. The protest was successful, but the plant was still installed a few years later. As a philosopher and an environmentalist, he believed in what he called "deep ecology". Ecology is the study of the relationship between living things and their environment. Naess's philosophy sees human life as just one of the many parts of Earth's total **ecosystem**, no more important than any other form of life.

The challenge of climate change

Global warming and the resulting climate change are the most serious environmental problems facing the world today. All green groups agree that this is an all-important challenge. They have concentrated on this issue in recent years, and there have been many books, magazine and newspaper articles, TV programmes, and even an Oscar-winning documentary film (called *An Inconvenient Truth*) on the subject.

According to the Climate Crisis website, the film "made global warming the number one topic of conversation". It concentrated on former US Vice President Al Gore's slide-show campaign to warn people about global warming. In 2007, a survey showed that two-thirds of people who saw the film said it had changed their mind about global warming by convincing them of the "inconvenient truth". Nearly 90 per cent said the film made them more aware of the problem – and nearly three-quarters said they changed some of their habits as a result.

Cause and effect of global warming

Global warming means a gradual rise in the overall temperature of the Earth. We know that our planet's temperature has gone up and down over many millions of years. There have been several long glacial periods (or ice ages). In the 20th and early 21st centuries, rising temperatures have been caused by human activities. These have added to the "greenhouse effect", which stops heat escaping from Earth in a similar way to glass trapping warmth inside a greenhouse. Certain gases in the atmosphere, such as carbon dioxide and **methane**, cause this effect. We have been adding enormously to them by emitting waste gases from power plants, factories, and cars. Scientists call this the "enhanced" greenhouse effect and environmentalists want to change the human activities that cause it.

When is a scientist an environmentalist?

The Intergovernmental Panel on Climate Change (IPCC) is the leading international organization for assessing and publishing scientific knowledge about global warming. Thousands of scientists from all over the world contribute to the work of the IPCC. They separate their scientific research from their own principles and beliefs, so that results and forecasts about the environment are factual and independent. Environmental science is their career. The views of environmentalists, on the other hand, are biased in favour of the environment. Scientist may also be environmentalists, but they keep their private views separate from their professional work.

The effect of global warming is shown clearly by melting ice in Alaska. In 1941, the Muir Glacier filled the photograph (above). By 2004, the glacier ended at the top of the shot (below).

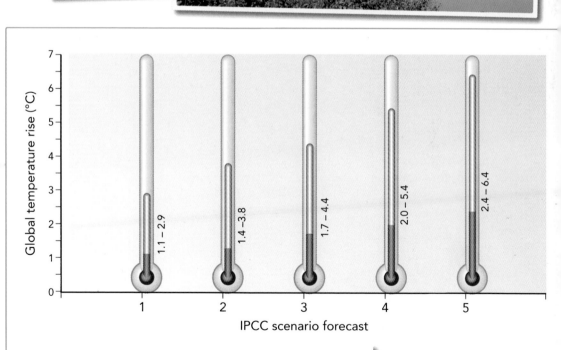

The bars show five different forecasts made by IPCC scientists for the rise in global temperature by 2100. They show the different low (1) and high (5) scenarios. The difference in numbers might seem small, but the difference in effects on life on Earth would be enormous.

PLANS AND EFFECTS

Like environmental scientists, environmental planners are professional people. They are usually responsible for individual practical projects. They work for local government agencies or private companies, helping them to make plans for developments such as buildings, factories, or harbours. These plans need to take the natural environment into account. Planners have to balance **developers**' wishes with environmental considerations.

At national level

The governments of all countries face similar challenges in balancing the short-term wishes of their citizens with long-term care for the health of the environment. Here are some examples of government departments around the world.

- Australia: Department of **Sustainability**, Environment, Water, Population and Communities
- Canada: Environment Canada
- China: Ministry of Environmental Protection
- New Zealand: Ministry for the Environment
- United Kingdom: Department for Environment, Food and Rural Affairs (Defra)
- United States: Environmental Protection Agency (EPA)

They all have different systems, laws, and ways of doing things, but they all include protection of the environment among their aims.

Roads have an enormous impact on the landscape. This motorway cuts through the Dutch countryside.

Environmental impact assessment

At national, regional, and local level, most countries make developers produce an **environmental impact assessment**. They must present this before going ahead with any development, so that government, councils, and individuals have a chance to react to it. This means that environmentalists can have an important say on developments – if necessary, encouraging authorities to turn them down.

The statement must describe the effects of a proposed development on the natural and physical environment. The "impact" is the changes caused by the development. The statement usually describes ways in which any unwanted impact may be avoided or lessened. Assessments are made for all kinds of developments, such as shopping centres and buildings, roads and railways, mines, factories, and other industrial sites.

Then and Now
View from the motorway

Germany is famous for having created the first Autobahn (motorway). The first road to be given this name was the 20-kilometre (12-mile) Autobahn between Cologne and Bonn that opened in 1932. The network grew quickly throughout Germany, and the new, fast roads passed beautiful countryside, including picturesque lakes and mountains. In the 1930s, motorway planners were mainly concerned with the landscape from the point of view of drivers of speeding cars. It was as if the planners and motorists were on the same side. Civil engineers were keen to show that they had the technology to build efficient, eye-pleasing bridges and tunnels. Things are very different in the 21st century, when environmentalists are more concerned with limiting how many roads and cars can be seen in the landscape.

Approval or refusal?

Detailed plans are usually made before a development application is made to local, regional, or national authorities. The authority might ask for further information and an environmental impact assessment. It might take years before a decision is reached, allowing local people plenty of time to comment and possibly object. Environmental groups may try to influence locals if they believe there are issues that they are not aware of. But the authorities take account of the NIMBY ("not in my back yard") effect, which leads people to object to something in their neighbourhood that they would happily see located elsewhere.

The European Landscape Convention

This convention (or international agreement), which came into force in 2000, promotes the protection, management, and planning of European landscapes. It defines the landscape as "part of the land, as perceived by local people or visitors, which evolves through time as a result of being acted upon by natural forces and human beings". The convention encourages the general public to take an active part in its aims, which means that green-thinking people can have an influence.

Approved: Tasmanian pulp mill

In the Tamar Valley of Tasmania, Australia, a private company proposed building a pulp mill, which processes wood fibre for making paper, calling it "the world's greenest pulp mill". However, in 2007, the Australian Environment Minister asked for an environmental impact plan to be made. The company was asked to show how it would limit discharge from the mill into the Tamar River and Bass Strait. It was also asked to use plantation-grown wood only for the fibres, and to use a more eco-friendly bleaching (or whitening) process. A proposed pipeline also had to take a different route.

When the revised plan included all these changes, the Environment Minister approved the development in 2011. But this may not be the end of the matter. The Tasmanian Greens group are running a campaign called Pulp the Mill. They say that there are still problems of air and noise pollution, as well as a negative impact on coastal waters. The Australian Wilderness Society agrees with the Greens.

Like other manufacturing plants, pulp and paper mills have a big impact on the environment. This mill was built beside a river in Florida, USA.

Refused: Oregon gold dredging

The Chetco River in southern Oregon, USA, was given environmental protection in 1988 as a "wild and scenic river". It flows through a wilderness area in the Rogue River–Siskiyou National Forest, which is managed by the US Forest Service. A gold-mining developer applied for a permit to use suction dredges to mine for gold in the fast-flowing river. These dredges are powerful machines that suck up rocks and gravel from the riverbed for processing on the surface. Any small pieces of gold are separated before the gravel is returned to the river. But the Oregon Department of Environmental Quality's rules on water quality ban activities that cause muddiness in salmon rivers such as the Chetco. So, in 2011, the application was turned down.

ENVIRONMENTALISM IN ACTION

Mining in the "Ore Mountains"

The Erzgebirge (German for "Ore Mountain Range") stretches for 160 kilometres (100 miles) along the border between Germany and the Czech Republic. Silver was first found there more than 800 years ago, and in the **Middle Ages**, mines opened and villages grew nearby. This changed the landscape, especially when other metals were discovered, including copper, lead, and tin.

Then and Now
Sustainable development

Hans Carl von Carlowitz (1645–1714) was born in Saxony and became a silver-mining supervisor. German historians call him "the inventor of sustainability" (development that does not use up resources). He saw that the forests of the Erzgebirge were being completely destroyed because so much wood was needed for the mining industry. Carlowitz wrote a book on how to make forestry sustainable by collecting seeds, preparing soil properly, and managing forests.

In the late 18th century, uranium was found in a mineral called pitchblende. During the 20th century, people started to use radioactive uranium as fuel for nuclear reactions, and then the metal became very important. After 1945, when East Germany was part of the **Soviet bloc**, uranium was useful to Russia for its nuclear weapons programme.

Reshaping the landscape

In 1991, the unified German government took over the company that ran the mines. They stopped mining and set about restoring the landscape. They had to close 9 underground mines and 1,400 kilometres (870 miles) of open mine workings. They had to deal with 311 million cubic metres (11 billion cubic feet) of waste rock from the mines and 160 million cubic metres (5.7 billion cubic feet) of radioactive **tailings** (waste left after ore is extracted from rock).

The Lichtenberg opencast mine made a vast hole 240 metres (787 feet) deep. This photograph was taken in 1990, after mining for uranium had stopped and waste material from nearby mines had been dumped at the site.

The Lichtenberg site, photographed in 2010, shows the reshaped land after the mine was filled in. The surface was covered with a layer of good soil 1.6 metres (5.2 feet) thick.

More than 20 years' work

Workers had to fill underground holes, cover old dumps, and demolish mine buildings. Many open mines were flooded, to make ponds and lakes, and all mine water had to be treated so that it did not pollute the new landscape. When work is finished at each site, soil is placed over bare areas, and trees and grass are planted. The German Ministry of Economics and Technology says that in the former mine region of the Erzgebirge, "Today's scenery is dominated by reclaimed landscapes".

Altogether, workers had to return approximately 37 square kilometres (14.3 square miles) of abandoned land to productive use. This was an enormous environmental clean-up job. Work started in 1992 and should be completed by 2015, at a total cost of €6.6 billion (£5.9 billion).

Land rehabilitation

Environmental planners call the sort of work done in the Erzgebirge "land rehabilitation" (restoring land to its earlier condition). This is common in former mining areas. As part of the plan, a mine is sometimes left as a tourist attraction. This has been done in some parts of the Erzgebirge with old tin and **tungsten** mines. You can even visit a mine that was first worked in 1558.

Disastrous effects

Natural and man-made disasters can have huge effects on the landscape. Environmentalists try to learn from these disasters and make plans to avoid them in future. The tsunami that hit Japan in 2011 is an example of a natural disaster that devastated the landscape.

The 2010 Gulf of Mexico oil spill was a man-made disaster that came about from an explosion on a drilling rig, which killed 11 workers. The oil company involved, BP, said that it regretted damage caused to the environment and was taking "measures to help ensure it does not happen again". The leaked oil did enormous damage to the Gulf coastline, and environmentalists are demanding that offshore oil drilling be stopped.

Impact on wildlife

Human development and natural and man-made disasters can have a devastating effect on wildlife, too. This was the case with the Gulf of Mexico oil spill. Tourism and leisure activities also have a big impact in rural locations. For example, they can divide natural habitats into patches too small to support healthy communities of wildlife.

One way to overcome this division of habitats is by creating **wildlife corridors**. A successful example is the fenced corridor built across a golf course in Jasper National Park, Canada. This was put up in 2001 to allow wolves and elk to move through their natural habitat, and it has been a great success.

A golf course is fringed by lakes and trees in Jasper National Park, Canada. Studies show that wild animals adapted quickly to the corridor that was built to allow them greater movement.

Landfills and the landscape

A landfill is a site where waste material is buried under soil. Household rubbish that is not suitable for recycling is generally taken to a landfill. The site may start off as a hole in the ground and end up as a large hill dominating its surroundings. Landfills are usually close to urban areas, where the waste is created, but they may also be next to countryside, rivers, or other landforms.

Landfills are always of great interest to environmentalists, who would like as much waste as possible to be reused or recycled. Since this is not always possible, they have put pressure on authorities to locate and operate landfills sensibly. In the United States, for example, the government's Environmental Protection Agency (EPA) says its plan "prevents the siting of landfills in environmentally-sensitive areas". The EPA says that landfills must be: built away from wetlands or flood plains; lined with a synthetic covering; and covered frequently with a layer of soil. Of course reducing the number and size of landfill sites makes them more expensive to use. This puts up the cost to businesses and public authorities, which in turn encourages them to reduce their waste.

Landfill laws

Environmentalists have succeeded in getting many regulations put in place regarding landfills. In the **European Union (EU)**, for example, the Landfill Directive sets rules to prevent the pollution of water, soil, and air, as well as emissions of methane. The directive aims to promote the recycling of rubbish and bans certain types of waste from being put in landfill sites, such as used tyres. By 2016, EU member states must reduce the amount of **biodegradable** waste they put in landfill to 35 per cent of their 1995 levels. In 2007, the EU started legal action against 14 of its member states for not making these regulations part of their national laws.

ENVIRONMENTALISM IN ACTION

Fresh Kills landfill

One of the largest landfill sites in the world opened on Staten Island, a borough of New York City, USA, in 1948. It started off as a small dump and was intended to last for just 20 years. It was called the Fresh Kills landfill, because it was located beside an **estuary** of the same name. (*Kill* is an old Dutch word for "riverbed" or "channel".)

The location was originally made up of marshland, and the landfill grew to cover 890 hectares (2,200 acres), nearly three times bigger than New York City's Central Park and covering more than one-twentieth of the island's area. Up to 20 barges of waste carried more than 26,000 tonnes of waste to the landfill every day from other parts of New York. The mounds of 136 million tonnes of solid waste rose up to 70 metres (200 feet). The landfill eventually closed in 2001. Most of New York City's garbage is now shipped to faraway landfills in the US states of New Jersey, South Carolina, and Virginia.

Reclaiming the land

The process of landfill reclamation has become more important as sites have grown beyond their originally intended size. Also, environmentalists have convinced many local authorities that large landfills are ruining the landscape. In the case of Fresh Kills, a plan was put together to reclaim the land and use it as a park. An environmental impact assessment (see page 17) was made, and it was published for public comments in 2008. The mounds of waste will be covered with six layers: a soil barrier, gas vent (see "Useful waste gas", opposite), waterproof liner, drainage, barrier protection, and – right on top – a layer of soil for plants.

Plans for the park

Landscape architects have planned for some of the land to be returned to tidal creeks, wetlands, meadows, grassland, and woodland. By 2014, there will be paths for hikers, cyclists, mountain bikers, and horse riders. The New York City Department of Parks and Recreation says, "The park's design, ecological restoration, and cultural and educational programming will emphasize environmental sustainability and a renewed public concern for our human impact on the Earth." The total development of the new Fresh Kills Park will take 30 years.

Landfill was stacked high at Fresh Kills (above) until it was closed in 2011. The cleared area (below) will become a recreational park.

Useful waste gas

Decomposing waste gives off methane, which is a powerful **greenhouse gas**. Whilst Fresh Kills Park is being designed and built, the methane is collected and used to heat about 20,000 homes. This will continue until there is only a little gas left, and then it will be burned off at special flare stations.

Architecture award

A similar, smaller landfill reclamation project near Barcelona, Spain, won an award at the World Architecture Festival in 2008. The judges said that the Spanish project was "a perfect example of bringing dead nature back to life by converting rubbish into a beautiful piece of landscape architecture". Perhaps Fresh Kills will be just as successful.

WORKING FOR THE ENVIRONMENT

The increasing importance and impact of environmentalism have created a wide range of new technologies and jobs. People with the right qualifications and experience can work for governments, local authorities, non-governmental organizations (NGOs), environmental groups, and charities, as well as private companies. This is an expanding field, and it is very likely that more opportunities will become available in future to work for the environment.

Local government

In the industrialized world, cities, towns, and boroughs usually have at least one special department to deal with environmental issues. The department may be called "Environment and planning", for example, and list as some of its responsibilities air quality, building control, conservation, **contaminated** land, energy efficiency, environmental health, planning, street cleaning, waste disposal, and recycling. There may be a separate department dealing with parks and recreation, or water quality and supply. Many local authorities have staff that put together and publish their plans and aims about cutting **carbon emissions** and encouraging sustainability.

An environmental inspector checks mud cracks in a drought region of California, USA. Lack of rain caused the land to dry up completely.

Educational qualifications

Because environmentalism covers such a wide area, many school courses are helpful to a budding environmentalist. Useful subjects include sciences such as biology, geography, geology, and ecology. As in many other jobs, writing, research, and computer skills are important.

There are various courses in higher education that can lead to a degree in environmental science or environmental studies. Environmental technology deals specifically with the application of scientific knowledge and engineering to solve environmental problems.

Variety of jobs

Committed environmentalists may become scientists, engineers, conservationists, researchers, journalists, or campaigners. They may work in a laboratory or an office, or carry out much of their work outdoors. As well as earth sciences, conservation, and ecology, there are specialist fields such as energy efficiency, environmental law and regulations, fisheries and wildlife management, food and farming, pollution control, sustainable transport, and waste management and recycling.

Today, it is increasingly important that those working in other fields have knowledge of green issues. This applies to architects, designers, planners, and builders, because they must all think about the sustainable nature of their materials and plans. Journalists and others in the media must also be aware of green issues.

Golf management

According to the Organic Consumers Association, "America's golf courses are devastating the environment." Environmentalists in many countries agree that golf courses take up far too much land, where they reduce **biodiversity** and change the landscape (for the better, say golfers). Golf courses need vast amounts of water and are often treated with fertilizers and pesticides. However, degree courses in golf course management now stress sustainability, giving students the opportunity to reduce golf's impact on the landscape.

The main UK golfing committee, the R&A, says it is working towards sustainable development by: "Optimising the playing quality of the golf course in harmony with the conservation of its natural environment under economically sound and socially responsible management".

United Nations programmes

Many environmental groups are funded by donations. Like all **United Nations (UN)** programmes, the United Nations Environment Programme (UNEP) is funded by its member states.

> "To provide leadership and encourage partnership in caring for the environment by inspiring, informing, and enabling nations and peoples to improve their quality of life without compromising that of future generations."
>
> UNEP mission

In recent years, one of UNEP's greatest success stories was helping more than 100,000 people in India to install solar panels for electricity in their homes. UNEP's headquarters are in Nairobi, Kenya. It has 1,185 staff working in 35 locations around the world. A much smaller UN department is the Convention to Combat **Desertification** (UNCCD), with headquarters in Bonn, Germany, and 60 staff in six locations.

Green days

The United Nations supports special days each year in an aim to increase awareness of green issues:

- 22 April – International Mother Earth Day (organized by the UN)
- 5 June – World Environment Day (UNEP)
- 17 June – World Day to Combat Desertification (UNCCD).

UNEP chose India to host its special day in 2011. The Programme is working to protect forests around the world.

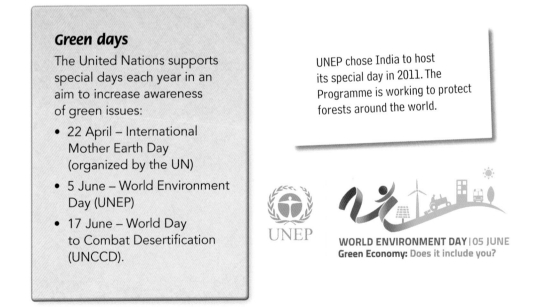

UNEP

WORLD ENVIRONMENT DAY | 05 JUNE
Green Economy: Does it include you?

Publicity

The main aim of special days is publicity. Books, magazine and newspaper articles, films, and television programmes all encourage people to think about the environment. Many products are endorsed and publicized by celebrities, and the same approach can be taken to the environment.

In 2011, the film star Cate Blanchett appeared in a TV commercial calling on Australians to back a tax on carbon, which she called a "price on pollution". The commercial gained a lot of publicity around the world, and shortly after it was shown, 45,000 people took part in "Australia Says Yes" rallies. The campaign was successful, and the Australian government announced that the country's biggest polluters will have to start paying a tax on their carbon emissions.

Theory versus practice

To environmentalists or **ecotourists**, the view of a natural, unspoiled landscape will always appear beautiful. For example, they would see the Brazilian rainforest or the Canadian boreal forest that way. The people who live in these regions would probably agree about their beauty, but at the same time they might take a more practical view.

Many people are dependent on local resources, such as wood, and these form part of the "unspoiled landscape". They need to use their environment's resources and opportunities, but they may well do so in a sustainable way. This is especially true in developing countries. So does this mean there is a conflict between green and realistic views, or between theory and practice? Not necessarily. It is the job of the practical environmentalist to overcome the problems of local economies. The caring environmentalist must always take local conditions and, especially, local people into consideration.

James Lovelock

The British chemist and environmentalist James Lovelock (born 1919) proposed his Gaia **hypothesis** (or proposed explanation) in the 1970s. Gaia (the ancient Greek goddess of the Earth) is Lovelock's name for our planet, which he sees as a global ecosystem that regulates itself and has the ability to keep itself healthy.

In 2006, Lovelock published a book called *The Revenge of Gaia*, in which he explained that humankind has exploited the Earth without counting the cost. Now global warming and climate change are signs that the Earth is fighting back. Some other scientists disagree with these controversial ideas.

FORESTS AND DESERTS

The world's forests and deserts form a major part of our global landscape. Forests cover more than one-quarter of the world's land area and play an important role in regulating Earth's climate. This is because, like all plants, trees take in carbon dioxide. They also help produce rainfall, because water evaporation is higher over forests than over cleared land.

The world's deserts, where rainfall is less than 25 centimetres (10 inches) a year, cover about one-fifth of land, and they are growing. Experts say that desertification (fertile land turning to desert) affects one-third of the Earth's surface and the lives of more than one billion people.

Double minus

Desertification and **deforestation** (the clearing of forests) are environmental disasters. They are both linked to climate change. When forests are cleared, much of the felled wood is burned as fuel. This releases carbon dioxide into the atmosphere, adding to global warming. It has been estimated that 30 per cent of the carbon dioxide added to the atmosphere over the past 150 years came from deforestation. Environmentalists point out that **afforestation** (turning land into forest) could help to limit global warming.

Forests and deserts are not usually right next to each other, but cutting down forests leads to their replacement by grassland. Poor land management (overgrazing by animals and overuse for cultivation) also causes soil to degrade and could lead to land becoming desert.

Then and Now
Easter Island

This small South Pacific island is famous for its gigantic stone statues. These were carved and put up by the native people in the years 1200–1700, when the island's population may have grown to about 15,000. They cut down trees to clear land for farming, and used logs to make canoes and build slides for dragging the heavy statues from the stone quarry. When there were no more trees, the land became barren, the population fell, there was civil war, and the islanders that were left faced a difficult future.

Today, Easter Island is a **UNESCO World Heritage Site**, with a population of less than 4,000. Historians and geographers quote the collapse of its civilization as an extreme and early example of the effects of deforestation.

This map shows that there is a risk of desertification on all continents. The very high-risk (red) areas are next to existing deserts.

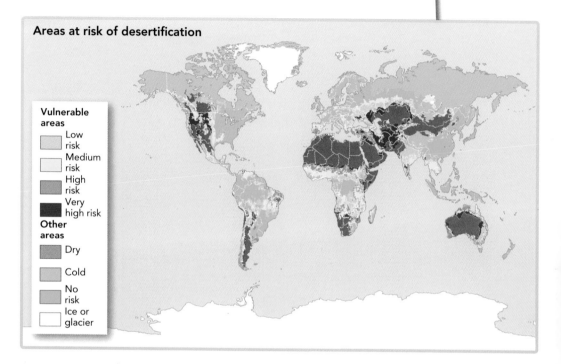

Areas at risk of desertification

Vulnerable areas
- Low risk
- Medium risk
- High risk
- Very high risk

Other areas
- Dry
- Cold
- No risk
- Ice or glacier

Desert landscape

"The climatic extremes of deserts have created a wide range of landscapes. ... Deserts provide us with some of the most spectacular and stunning scenery on the planet. From the dramatic rock formations of Death Valley in the USA, to the sand dunes of the Sahara, the world's arid zones constitute a natural gift that should be neither overlooked nor taken for granted."

Oxfam's "Cool Planet" website

Oxfam says that 13 per cent of the world's population live in deserts. Do you think many of those people would agree with the description of their landscape?

ENVIRONMENTALISM IN ACTION

Iron-ore mining in Western Australia

Four deserts stretch across large parts of the state of Western Australia:
the Great Sandy Desert, Little Sandy Desert, Great Victoria Desert,
and Gibson Desert. Iron ore is the state's most important mineral,
and 97 per cent of the country's total iron is mined and produced
there. The state capital Perth is Australia's mining capital.

The country is the second largest producer of iron ore in the world (see
table below). More than 90 per cent of Australia's ore is exported, and
about two-thirds go to China. But this is still not enough iron for the
world's biggest steel-maker, China, which is estimated to have less
than half the amount of usable reserves of iron ore as Australia.

Iron ore produced in 2010		
Country	Millions of tonnes	Percentage of world production
China	900	38
Australia	420	18
Brazil	370	15
India	260	11
Russia	100	4

Leasing land

As well as buying Australian iron ore, Chinese companies are
leasing huge areas of land in the north-west of the country. They are
developing their own vast **opencast mines**, along with processing
plants and on-site power stations, and even building a new port, from
which to ship their ore home. China expects to ship 2 billion tonnes of
iron ore over the next 25 years. This looks like a good deal for China,
and many Australians are happy, too. One of the benefits for Australia,
in addition to income from the lease, is that the project will create
thousands of jobs for Australian workers.

The iron-ore mine has its own gas-fired power station. This generates electricity to drive enormous crushing and grinding machines, which separate the ore from rock and turn it into pellets.

Environmental management plan

The Chinese-owned mining company says that it has "a strong commitment to sustainable mining practices that minimize impacts on the natural environment". It has put together an extensive environmental management plan. The plan says that the company's on-site power station will produce 40 per cent less greenhouse gas emissions than other plants. The company also intends to build a **desalination** plant on the coast, to turn seawater into fresh water, so that the iron-ore mines will not use up precious fresh water supplies. Many of these positive developments came about because of environmental impact assessment requirements put forward by the Australian Environmental Protection Authority some years ago.

Cultural impact

Impact on the landscape can be cultural as well as environmental. In the case of Western Australia, the red-tinged rocks, desert, and bush are full of archaeological evidence that means a great deal to the country's Aboriginal people.

The Aborigines have lived in Australia for at least 40,000 years. Their present-day leaders are unhappy that their sacred lands might be dug up or used as a dump for mine tailings. One ancient Aboriginal ochre (a rust-coloured mineral clay) mine was first worked at least 10,000 years ago. The chief executive of the Chinese mining company has assured Australians that important Aboriginal sites will not be touched.

Restoring forests

Since they began campaigning for change, environmentalists have always made forests a top priority. They have pushed for **reforestation** (replanting of trees) and afforestation (converting land into forest). Today, Greenpeace is campaigning for zero deforestation across the world (no clearing of forests at all) by 2020. Their campaigners want to "inspire consumer action to demand that our food, paper, and timber products aren't linked to forest destruction". Their efforts have had an impact in practical ways, such as the use of properly harvested wood.

Forest Stewardship Council

The Forest Stewardship Council (FSC) is a non-profit organization that promotes responsible management of the world's forests. It **certifies** more than 1.2 million square kilometres (463,000 square miles) of forest in over 80 countries around the world. The Council lends its name to well-managed forests and adds its logo to wood products and paper that are made from trees harvested in the least damaging way. This helps consumers choose the most sustainable products.

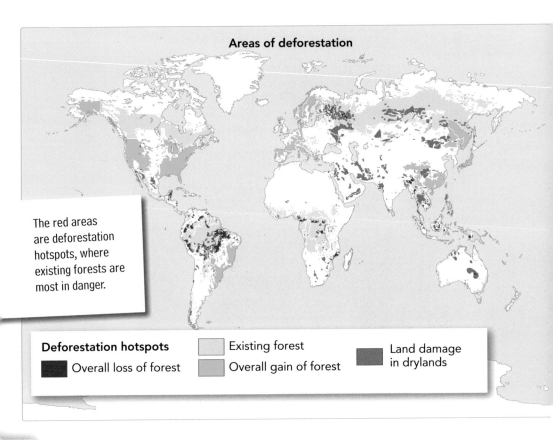

Areas of deforestation

The red areas are deforestation hotspots, where existing forests are most in danger.

Deforestation hotspots	Existing forest	Land damage in drylands
Overall loss of forest	Overall gain of forest	

How many football pitches?

One way for environmentalists to influence opinion is to quote statistics that people can easily understand and relate to their own lives. This is what Friends of the Earth say about deforestation:

"Around 1.6 billion people rely on forests in some way. Forests are disappearing at an incredible rate – we're losing an area of forest the size of 36 football pitches per minute."

Making forest law

In May 2011, Brazil's government voted to change their forest laws and ease restrictions on the amount of land farmers must preserve as forest. This would reduce the amount of land that must be left unharmed along the banks of rivers and streams from 30 metres (100 feet) to 15 metres (50 feet).

Environmental groups objected in an attempt to influence the Brazilian president, who has the power to overturn the decision. They say that the Amazon forest has never been as threatened as it is now. But farmers are rushing to cut down forests, hoping that the new law will protect them from wrongdoings in the past. So, farmers want to do one thing, and environmentalists another. Laws may depend on who has the greatest influence on politicians.

Then and Now
From medieval forestry to modern forest management

In the Middle Ages, people protected forests to provide deer for noblemen to hunt. In England, there were laws to protect royal forests, which also provided timber for ships. By the 16th century, foresters in France and the German states were starting to plant new trees to replace those cut down. Two hundred years later, French and German universities were teaching forestry. Today, forest management is a more scientific subject, and students take a greener view of forestry. There are specialist universities, such as the Yale School of Forestry and Environmental Studies (USA), Edinburgh School of Forestry (UK), and Melbourne Department of Forest and Ecosystem Science (Australia).

ENVIRONMENTALISM IN ACTION

Problems of the Sahel

The Sahel is a region of dry grassland that stretches right across Africa. It lies just to the south of the Sahara Desert, and its name comes from the Arabic for "shore", because it borders the desert. Since 1968, the region has suffered severe droughts, killing millions of people. Rainfall continued to decrease throughout the 1970s. Drought and overgrazing by animals led to desertification.

Keita Project

The Keita Valley is in south-west Niger, in the middle of the Sahel. It covers an area of 4,860 square kilometres (1,880 square miles) and is dominated by a plateau and rocky slopes. In the early 1960s, these slopes were covered by forest. By 1972, there were signs of forest degradation, and 12 years later the forest had almost completely disappeared. By then, environmentalists had decided to try and save the area, and the Keita Project began. It was financed by the Italian government and carried out by the UN's Food and Agriculture Organization. Its aim was to change the landscape of barren earth into a productive area of trees and other plants.

The load on this boy's donkey shows how successfully plants have grown again in the Keita Valley.

Changing the landscape

Workers used ploughing machines to cut holes in the rock-hard ground. Agronomists (specialists in soil management and crop production) managed the work of planting trees, digging wells, and making supply roads. Over 19 years, they planted 18.7 million trees, reclaiming and improving 345 square kilometres (133 square miles) of barren land.

They saw the new woodlands grow to three times the previous size, and the production of cereal grasses went up by 40 per cent. The local population grew from 65,000 in 1962 to 230,000 forty years later. This reversed the trend of increasing numbers of "climate refugees" – people who flee environmental problems caused by changes in climate.

Successful effects

Not only has the Keita Project been a success, experts also believe that the experience and data gained will help similar projects in the Sahel and elsewhere. They know that such projects must last decades, since it may take much longer for land to recover than it does for it to degrade. Prevention would certainly be less costly than cure.

They also calculated that the Keita Valley now removes 120,000 tonnes of carbon dioxide from the atmosphere every year. That's about the amount of carbon dioxide that 23,000 cars produce in a year. Perhaps this successful project shows one way forward in the battle against global warming.

Forest gardens

Forest gardens are areas of land planted with trees and bushes that produce fruits, nuts, herbs, and vegetables. They are popular in many parts of the developing world, such as India and Indonesia in Asia, and Tanzania and Kenya in Africa. Farmers realize that trees help keep their land fertile as well as providing food, fodder, and fuel. Environmentalists encourage these practices, both in developing and industrialized countries. In the United States, for example, more than one-third of forest land is owned and managed by millions of families and individuals known as "family forest owners".

COASTS AND RIVERS

The world's coasts and rivers are constantly changing, though often by small amounts over long periods of time. The moving water of seas and rivers wears away rocks, in a process called erosion. This affects the surrounding landscape.

Environmentalists and specialists in coastal and river management have learned that attempts to stop this natural process generally only succeed in pushing the problem elsewhere. Rising sea levels will change the landscape even more, as areas near coasts and river deltas are flooded. In the short term, many environmentalists have been most concerned about reducing pollution in these sensitive areas.

Coastal management

Since coastal erosion is a natural process, should we do anything about it or simply let nature take its course? Some environmentalists might argue that the "do nothing" approach is the greenest option. But others might reply that the landscape is changing anyway, so it is reasonable to change things even more for the benefit of people. We used to talk about "coastal defence", as if a hostile sea was invading the land. The more environmental approach has led to the term "coastal management". This allows us to work more with the sea than against it.

On this beach in Barcelona, Spain, a ship dredges (scoops up) sand from the seabed. It then pumps the sand through a hose on to land. This is a form of beach nourishment.

Rising sea level

At a UN climate conference in 2010, the world's governments agreed to try to hold the increase in global average temperature below 2°C (3.6°F). Even at this level of increase, coastal flooding is predicted to affect millions of people around the world.

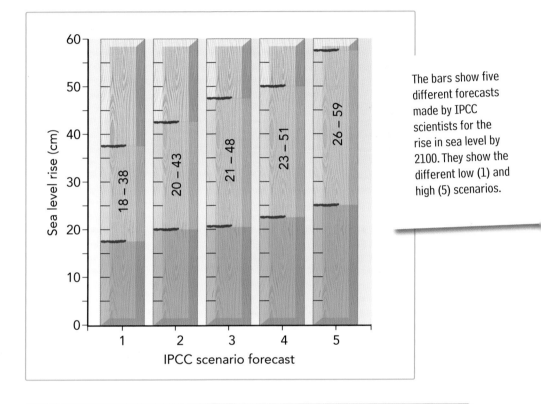

The bars show five different forecasts made by IPCC scientists for the rise in sea level by 2100. They show the different low (1) and high (5) scenarios.

Taking the soft option

"Hard engineering" techniques try to control erosion by creating barriers. These might be sea walls, groynes (wooden barriers built out into the sea), gabions (wire cages filled with rocks), or breakwaters. These were all common during the first half of the 20th century. Today, coastal managers often take a more sustainable approach, called "soft engineering". This might involve beach nourishment: making beaches higher and wider by importing sand and shingle to an area affected by longshore drift. It could mean stabilizing cliffs by covering them in matting or vegetation to resist erosion. Or it could mean accepting a managed retreat, allowing an area of coast to erode naturally, moving people and losing buildings. This keeps the natural balance and encourages the development of beaches and **salt marshes**.

ENVIRONMENTALISM IN ACTION

Fast-eroding coastline

The Holderness coastal region of East Yorkshire in north-west England has one of the fastest eroding shorelines in Europe. The 50-kilometre-(30-mile-) long coast is made up of soft boulder clay (hardened mud and sand), which was deposited there by glaciers during the last Ice Age up to 18,000 years ago. The cliffs are up to 35 metres (115 feet) high in places, but they are eroding fast, at an average of 1.7 metres (5½ feet) a year. Since Roman times (1st–5th centuries), 30 coastal villages have been lost to the North Sea.

Longshore drift

Strong waves approach the Holderness coast from the north-east, but the tidal currents of the North Sea flow in a southerly direction. This means that eroded clay from the cliffs is driven south along the coast, in a process called longshore drift (because material is driven along the shore). Every year about 1 million cubic metres (35 million cubic feet) of clay are eroded from the cliffs.

Coastal erosion has caused landslides near the village of Aldbrough on the Holderness coast. Nearby buildings are under threat and caravans will soon have to move.

At the southern end of the coast, where it meets the wide estuary of the River Humber, the drift has created a **spit** called Spurn Head. From about 6,000 years ago, erosion has removed part of this spit, and then rebuilt it again, in a 250-year cycle. The last breach of the spit was in 1849, before coastal protection works began. Experts think that the spit will soon be breached again.

Passing the problem on

Geographers will tell you that the trouble with trying to manage coasts, rivers, and many other landforms is that a problem solved in one place simply passes on to another. And this is true of Holderness. The sea walls, groynes, rock armour, and other devices have slowed local erosion to villages, but have created more erosion to either side of the defences. They have also slowed the movement of sediment to the Humber estuary and North Lincolnshire coast, leaving the land there less fertile. So what is to be done? The local authorities are trying to hold the line near villages that are already protected by updating hard defences. Elsewhere, they are allowing natural processes to take their course.

Environmental impact

Erosion clearly has a great impact on the coastal landscape. Our "hard engineering" solutions also have a short-term impact, both on the landscape and erosion. But benefits in one area can have a negative effect in another. Green influence has led to a softer approach, which in this case leads to a more natural impact.

Designed protection

If you have to put up a sea wall, then it can at least look as good as possible. In 2004, a 550-metre- (1,800-foot-) long stone-faced reinforced concrete wall was built to protect a beach and village on the Isle of Wight, off the south coast of England. As well as planners, engineers, designers, builders, and many others, the scheme included John Maine, a well-known Royal Academy sculptor. In his own work, Maine explores sculpture in relation to landscape, and he contributed to the artistic qualities of the sea wall design.

River flood protection

Like coasts, rivers are difficult to control. The main cause of flooding beside rivers is too much rain in too short a time. Scientists and engineers cannot change the weather, but many attempts have been made to protect land, especially towns, from flooding. River channels have been deepened, and riverbanks have been strengthened and heightened by earth or concrete **levees** (embankments). Dams have been built to hold back water, reservoirs to contain it, and spillways to provide overflow areas. But still major floods occur regularly. As with coasts, the softer environmentalist approach has become more popular.

Natural wetlands

Wetlands (marshes and swamps) act as sponges beside rivers, holding water and slowly releasing it. They are a natural flood control.

"Preserving and restoring wetlands, together with other water retention, can often provide the level of flood control otherwise provided by expensive dredge operations and levees. ... Wetlands along the Mississippi River once stored at least 60 days of floodwater. Now they store only 12 days because most have been filled or drained."

US Environmental Protection Agency

Green campaigners would like to see wetlands restored, changing the surroundings of many rivers into a more natural landscape.

"Over the last 200 years, around 475,000 square kilometres [183,000 square miles] of wetlands have been drained. These wetlands traditionally formed a buffer between the rivers and other low-lying lands, and their loss has meant that floodwaters became concentrated further downstream causing the floods. Public opinion is now leaning towards allowing the ex-wetlands (now mainly crop land) to flood again, so that area further downstream (with buildings, etc.) will be protected."

Green campaigner

Mississippi spillways

In 1927, there was a major flood along the Mississippi River in the United States. Since then, a lot of work has been done on building and rebuilding dams, levees, and other defences. Then, in 1993 and 2011, there were further serious floods, convincing many living near the river that still more defences had to be built.

Many environmentalists, on the other hand, believe that more spillways (or floodways) should be planned, so that the river can take a more natural course. This would flood farmers' land, causing them to lose their livelihood. During a serious flood in 2011, gates had to be opened to allow water into spillways. The flooded land divided opinion. Farmers and riverside house-owners were understandably annoyed, while others were glad that flooding of towns was avoided.

Waters of the Mississippi River flooded this farm in Missouri when a levee was blasted open in 2011. The flood affected at least 100 properties in the area.

"Safe environmentalists"?

In May 2011, the US Army Corps of Engineers blasted open a levee on the Mississippi River to protect the town of Cairo, Illinois. This flooded 530 square kilometres (205 square miles) of farmland. A politician wrote in the newspaper *USA Today*:

"Returning the river to its natural state represents a high ideal for environmentalists who live in safer places, but reducing flood protection is an unthinkable violation of property rights and liberty for Americans who have lived beside the river for more than a century."

Many farmers living alongside the river probably agreed with this criticism of the "idealistic" environmentalist view. What do you think?

ENERGY SOURCES

All the different ways in which we harness our world's energy have an effect on the landscape. Extracting fossil fuels (coal, oil, and gas) creates the visible impact of mines and spoil heaps. Their recovery and use also cause pollution and add to the greenhouse effect. Environmentalists have argued against fossil fuels for many years, and their efforts have reduced the impact on the environment to some extent. But the increasing use of renewable sources of energy can also affect the landscape. Green campaigners are struggling to convince everyone that the countryside is not being ruined by wind turbines and electricity pylons.

Dirty fuels

Greens call fossil fuels dirty because they cause so much pollution. In the United Kingdom, the terrible effects of London smog in 1952, which killed 4,000 people, led to new regulations about burning coal. People started to take air pollution seriously. During the 1960s, there was great concern about acid rain killing trees and putting whole forests at risk. Since people could easily see the effects of acid rain as they walked, cycled, or drove through forests of stripped trees, the environmentalist campaigns were very effective.

Can coal be clean?

Despite all the problems and the efforts of environmentalists, coal is still used to generate 41 per cent of the world's electricity. Some experts believe that "clean coal" techniques could reduce coal's impact on the landscape. The **carbon capture and storage (CCS)** process prevents carbon dioxide entering the atmosphere by removing it and storing it under ground. There are several projects around the world testing out this technique, but it is not yet in large-scale operation.

Whatever the results, many environmentalists are unconvinced. Greenpeace says:

"Coal is the dirtiest fuel there is and belongs in the past. Clean, inexpensive, renewable energy options already exist. This is where investment should be directed, rather than squandering valuable resources on a dirty dinosaur."

A drilling rig and a network of pipelines stand on the snow and ice of Alaska, USA. Energy companies want to drill for more gas and oil in the frozen Arctic region.

Putting an unspoiled landscape at risk

Oil rigs, drills, refineries, and especially oil spills – they all have their effect on the environment. Green groups highlight every oil spill, and there have been many such major catastrophes in recent years.

One especially threatened environment is the Arctic, where oil spills have done huge damage. Some companies even want to drill for oil in the Arctic National Wildlife Refuge in Alaska, the largest protected wilderness in the United States, but there is huge opposition. In June 2011, Greenpeace activists tried to stop drilling in the freezing seas off Greenland. The oil-drilling company then threatened to take the environmental group to court and apply for a fine of €2 million (£1.8 million) for every drilling day lost.

Arctic Council

It's not just green groups that fight against pollution and spoiled landscapes. In 1996 all countries with Arctic territory (Canada, Denmark, Finland, Iceland, Norway, Russia, Sweden, and the United States) got together to form the Arctic Council. One of the Council's main aims is to promote cooperation across the whole region on issues of sustainable development and environmental protection.

Is nuclear green?

"From an environmental perspective, nuclear energy can't be beaten. No belching smokestacks or polluting gases. … It also takes up hardly any land. One double-reactor plant takes up a few hundred acres and can power 2 million homes. The same production from wind or solar can take tens of thousands of acres, often blighting scenic views."

These words appeared in the *Washington Times* in January 2009. But nuclear energy impacts on the environment, as many greens will tell you. To begin with, uranium has to be mined to make nuclear fuel. Then there's the problem of radioactive nuclear waste: no one knows how to deal safely with this material, which is potentially very harmful to the environment. And thirdly, there's the question of safety. Major accidents at Chernobyl in the Ukraine in 1986 and at Fukushima in Japan in 2011 have highlighted the problem. It has been estimated that the Chernobyl disaster contaminated 150,000 square kilometres (58,000 square miles) of land.

Renewable impact

Some greens support nuclear energy, on the grounds that it is better (or less bad) than fossil fuels. But most are against nuclear and firmly in favour of renewable sources of energy. However, renewables have an effect on the landscape, too.

- *Biomass power*: using plant material for energy (such as in **biofuels**) means taking over a lot of land. In some parts of the world, this has caused deforestation and taken land away from food production; burning biomass causes pollution.

- *Geothermal power*: plants and pipelines are needed to use the internal heat of the Earth, and these would spoil landscapes in some of the world's volcanic regions; there have been protests against plans for one in a Hawaiian rainforest.

- *Solar power*: large-scale schemes need enormous amounts of land for collectors and reflectors; deserts are a good solar location, but ecosystems would suffer.

- *Water power*: hydroelectric schemes cause problems (see pages 48–52); tidal barrages and lagoons affect the coastline and its wildlife; **wave farms** affect shipping.

- *Wind power*: many people hate the sight and sound of turbines (see opposite).

Rows of turbines at a wind farm in California, USA, show how harvesting the wind has changed the look of the landscape. The state of California has more than 11,600 wind turbines.

Blot on the landscape?

Most greens are very enthusiastic about wind farms, while many people call them a blot on the landscape. Some see wind turbines as attractive examples of environmentally-friendly technology; others believe they ruin the countryside (or coasts if they are offshore). Who will win the argument?

Against wind turbines: They spoil the landscape.

For wind turbines: "Compared to mountain top removal from coal mining, oil extraction, nuclear power plants, and other energy developers, wind farms are quite elegant."

Greenpeace

Influencing public opinion

It is interesting to compare the general public's views with those of environmentalists. In a 2011 opinion poll, Americans were asked which of six energy sources they thought should be relied on more. The results were:

1. solar power   88 %
2. wind power   83 %
3. natural gas   70 %
4. coal   43 %
5. nuclear power   42 %
6. oil   28 %

Most environmentalists would agree with the top two. They would probably put coal down with oil. And many, but not all, would also mark down nuclear power. What influence do environmentalists have on public opinion?

ENVIRONMENTALISM IN ACTION

Three Gorges hydroelectric project

The world's largest hydroelectric scheme is being completed on the Chang Jiang (Yangtze River) in China. Building work on the huge dam began in 1994. The first electric generator started working in 2003, and by 2008 most of the hydroelectric plant was in operation. By 2011, extra generators were being tested and an enormous **ship elevator** was being built, to go along with the existing locks. The project should be completed by 2014. The plant's full generating power is 22,500 MW (8,500 MW more than the second most powerful dam, the Itaipu on the Brazil–Paraguay border).

China and renewables

China is the world's largest producer of electricity from renewable sources. Most comes from hydroelectric plants (most of the rest from wind), which generate 16 per cent of total electricity. China's State Energy Bureau has announced plans to nearly double its hydro-electric output by 2020, and much of this power will come from Three Gorges. However, China's booming economy still relies on coal, which is set to continue to supply more than two-thirds of the country's total energy. China also tops the world league of greenhouse gas producers, ahead of the United States and Indonesia.

The dam has power-generating sections to right and left. In the middle is a spillway, with gates that can be opened to let water through from the reservoir.

Three Gorges facts & figures

- The dam is 2,335 metres (7,661 feet) long.
- It is 181 metres (594 feet) high.
- The project used 27.2 million cubic metres (961 million cubic feet) of concrete.
- It used 463,000 tonnes of steel.
- About 103 million cubic metres (3,620 million cubic feet) of earth were moved.
- The reservoir is 660 kilometres (410 miles) long and 1.1 kilometres (0.7 mile) wide.
- It has a surface area of 1,045 square kilometres (404 square miles) and contains 39.3 cubic kilometres (9.4 cubic miles) of water.
- The reservoir water level is a maximum of 175 metres (575 feet) above sea level and 110 metres (360 feet) higher than the river level downstream.
- There are 32 generators, each producing 700 MW of electricity; plus two small generators (50 MW each); the total output is 22,500 MW.
- Two ship locks (see page 51) are made up of five stages, with a transit time of around four hours.
- The ship elevator will travel a vertical distance of 113 metres (370 feet), with a transit time of 30–40 minutes.

Moving people from their homes

The building of the dam – especially the creation of the reservoir, which filled up behind the dam – has had a huge impact on the local population. Around 1.4 million people have been forced to move from their homes, as more than 1,000 towns and villages were flooded. Some reports have suggested that many more people will have to move if environmental problems get worse.

Benefits of the scheme

The main purpose of Three Gorges is to generate electricity. The project has brought electricity to millions of villagers for the first time. Electricity generated by the dam is also sent along enormous transmission lines to cities such as Shanghai. The dam is also intended to help control flooding. The lower Chang Jiang has had many devastating floods, and the dam's reservoir has the capacity to hold extra water when necessary. This use was shown in 2009, when the dam held water back to reduce flooding downstream.

Dachang

The ancient town of Dachang was flooded by the Three Gorges reservoir. Before this happened, the town's three gates were taken down and ancient buildings and pillars were marked for reassembly before being moved. Then the town was rebuilt on a new site about 6 kilometres (4 miles) away. Some residents moved with the town, while others decided to move away. Local people hope that the "new" ancient town will still be a tourist attraction.

Three Gorges has become a tourist attraction. This is the visitor centre, which offers a good view of the dam.

The dam also has a benefit to shipping. The reservoir and widening of the river behind the dam allows larger ships to navigate the river further upstream. A series of locks and an elevator allows ships to pass the dam in both directions. The ship elevator is the large structure at the near end of the dam in the photograph on the opposite page. The locks are on the other side of the visitor centre.

Environmental problems

In 2011, the Chinese government warned that the Three Gorges region faced urgent environmental problems. The first is the danger of earthquakes and landslides, caused by the weight of extra water in the reservoir. This has been shown to be a problem at other dam sites around the world. Another problem is the storing of silt (or sediment) in the reservoir. This silt builds up the river's bed and banks further downstream, but the dam is stopping it. The reservoir has also had a build-up of **algae** and pollution. This will affect wildlife, and especially fish. Some reports say that the dam has contributed to drought downstream, though in 2011 more water was let through the dam to relieve drought.

To dam or not to dam the Nu

China had plans to build up to 13 dams on the River Nu, in Yunnan Province. This river flows through the Three Parallel Rivers National Park, which is a UNESCO World Heritage Site. In 2004, these plans were dropped after protests from Chinese environmental groups. But in 2011, a giant Chinese energy company announced new plans to dam the Nu for electricity, so the environmentalists will have to take up the challenge again.

A blueprint for the world?

Environmentalists are concerned that Three Gorges will act as a spur to other countries before the problems are fully understood or sorted out. In Turkey, for example, they fear that a rush to build hydroelectric schemes will add to the problem of desertification. One large project on the River Tigris will flood an ancient city and has caused huge controversy. Environmentalists are against the dam, but the Turkish government says the scheme will create thousands of jobs and help irrigate farmland.

TOWARDS ECOTOURISM

Since the 1970s, environmentalists have been concerned about the effects of mass tourism on the landscape. Figures show that in 1970 there were about 175 million international tourists. By 2005, this number had grown to more than 800 million, and many tourists were travelling to faraway places that they had read about in books and magazines.

However hard they try, it is difficult for tourists not to leave their mark on their destination. They inevitably create waste and pollution. This problem led to the idea of ecotourism, defined by the International Ecotourism Society as "responsible travel to natural areas that conserves the environment and improves the wellbeing of local people".

Mass tourism

"The Mexican Caribbean is comprised of magical places for an unforgettable holiday." So says a travel company that sells holidays on the Yucatán Peninsula, which they also call the Mayan Riviera, to make customers think of the French Riviera, a glamorous holiday destination. They encourage you to fly to Cancún, which just 40 years ago was a small fishing village on a deserted sand spit. By 2010, the resort had a population of 705,000 and received 5.9 million tourists. Many stay in the resort, but others travel down the Yucatán coast, which has seen huge development in recent years. This is an extreme case of tourist influence, but there are similar examples the world over.

Photographs like this present an image of the Yucatán coast as an unspoiled paradise. But what if it was full of tourists?

Minimizing impact

Ecotourists try to minimize their impact on the landscape, following the slogan, "Leave nothing but footprints". But this is easier said than done, since tourism often has unintended consequences.

The effects on coasts can be dramatic, as they can also be in the mountains. In the summer, ramblers can cause increased erosion, while in the winter, skiers and snowboarders encourage the building of roads, lifts, and hotels. The National Geographic Society suggests that sustainable tourism should leave destinations unspoiled for future generations. The Society promotes what it calls geotourism: "tourism that sustains or enhances the geographical character of a place – its environment, culture, aesthetics, heritage, and the well-being of its residents".

"Greenwashing"

In recent years, it has become common for travel companies, just like many manufacturers, to make claims about how environmentally friendly they are. But in some cases, this might be a marketing ploy to attract business, rather than a genuine attempt to "go green". Such ploys show how successful environmentalists have been in promoting the idea of ecotourism. The deceptive use of green claims is called **greenwashing**, and all sorts of companies use it.

Greenpeace is so concerned about greenwashing that it runs a special website (www.stopgreenwash.org), where examples are posted. They also highlight success stories, such as the French consumer protection agency, which ruled that cars should no longer be portrayed in nature, such as forests and beaches, but must only be shown on proper roads.

ENVIRONMENTALISM IN ACTION

Rainforest tourism

The destruction of rainforests is one of the biggest issues on the green agenda. So experience of this unique habitat is important. Here we look at some examples of successful ecotourism, all based in the forest. Which one do you think environmentalists would vote the best? And which would you choose for an exciting eco-holiday?

Wildlife conservation

According to UNESCO, tourism is largely responsible for saving the mountain gorillas of Rwanda from extinction. Farmers were clearing land, and poachers were killing wildlife. But the establishment of a tourist scheme to go on a "gorilla trek" in the Volcanoes National Park has brought in enough money to change the situation. Former Rwandan farmers are employed as park guards and guides. The Rwanda Development Board issues permits allowing groups of up to eight tourists to go with a guide and spend up to an hour close to the gorillas. There are seven gorilla families in the Park, and the largest contains 41 individuals. Rwanda Eco-Tours advises: "Gorilla permits sell out quickly. Reserve your permit 30 days before the planned tour date." As well as protecting the gorillas, this project contributes to looking after the Rwandan forest environment.

Victim of success?

Manuel Antonio National Park, in Costa Rica, was set up in 1972 to protect its beautiful environment. The park has rainforest, mangrove swamps, lagoons, and beaches. It is home to 109 different kinds of mammal and 184 bird species, attracting 200,000 visitors a year. The numbers would probably be even greater, but the authorities decided to limit visitors to 600 per day and close the park on Mondays. They were worried about overuse and the effect on the forest and its ecosystem. This shows how ecotourism can be a victim of its own success.

Perhaps there is too much on offer at Manuel Antonio. You can hire an all-terrain vehicle to drive around or use pulleys to travel across platforms high in the rainforest canopy. The park's website says, "The main objective is to provide tourists a unique activity and ecological experience while, at the same time, helping to aid in the preservation of the world's endangered rain forests through direct financial support to conservation, education, and reforestation efforts."

Manuel Antonio National Park lies on the Pacific coast of Costa Rica. The park's beaches are popular with tourists, who can enjoy horse riding and rambling, as well as swimming.

Brazilian ecotourist town

In the 1980s, the small number of inhabitants of Alta Floresta, at the edge of the Amazon rainforest in Brazil, were goldminers. Today, the town is best known as a centre of ecotourism. There is a research centre, where locals and visitors can study sustainable ways of using the forest. The School of the Amazon programme aims to teach ecological awareness to local teenagers as well as students from all over the world. There are lots of organized trips. Some are for birdwatchers, others for those generally interested in the largest rainforest in the world. There are special trips with expert guides to see spider monkeys and giant otters. Nearby there is a jungle lodge, where tourists can immerse themselves in the rainforest.

SUMMING IT UP

Environmentalist ideas have changed since the "back to nature" movement developed in the 19th century. Most green supporters are still concerned about conservation – that is, the protection of the natural environment, including its wilderness areas and wildlife. Today they add to this the important idea of sustainability – the preservation of an environmental balance by not allowing natural resources to be reduced and eventually used up.

These ideas have had a great effect on the way in which people think about and relate to our planet, especially its physical features. The landscape might still be under threat in many places, but without environmental awareness that threat might have been much worse.

Practical impact

Environmentalism has had a practical impact on the landscape in several ways. It has led people in all walks of life to look at the natural features as important, irreplaceable resources. This view has led to new attitudes towards the world's forests, for example – including a strong movement against deforestation. In the same way, scientists and politicians are combating large, global problems such as desertification.

Do electricity pylons ruin a landscape? Are they a good idea if they carry electricity to cities from renewable energy sources, such as wind turbines? This is a modern green dilemma.

At a more regional and local level, coastlines, rivers, and similar landscape features are affected and protected by modern green ideas. These tend to promote a softer approach with less intervention than previously. Environmental planners and managers are much more involved at all levels – global, national, regional, and local – than in earlier times.

Climate change

The results of climate change cause some of the most serious environmental problems facing the world today. Human activity has added to the greenhouse effect, which in turn causes global warming. Rising temperatures affect all landforms and increase the spread of desertification. The melting of polar ice caps leads to a rise in sea level that affects coasts and nearby land.

Environmentalists are trying to reduce these effects on the landscape by encouraging us all to help combat global warming. Many of their efforts are aimed at the energy sources we all rely on. Environmentalists stress that we must reduce our burning of fossil fuels, increase our use of renewable sources of energy, and use energy more efficiently.

Into the future

How will environmentalism develop in future? What effects will it have on the landscape? Obviously we can only speculate on the future, but it seems likely that the environmentalist influence will increase. The general public is much more aware of green issues than ever before, and this trend will surely continue. This awareness could lead to more pressure on politicians and others – people like us – to take action to protect our natural surroundings.

Getting involved

There are many ways to get involved with environmentalism. There are educational courses and many different kinds of jobs for scientists and others. Green groups and organizations welcome helpers and volunteers.

TIMELINE

This list adds other important entries to the dates of people and events mentioned in the book.

4th century BC Ancient Greek philosopher Plato describes deforestation.

1645–1714 Life of Hans Carl von Carlowitz, called "the inventor of sustainability" by German historians.

1825 Schools of forestry are set up in Germany and France.

1834–1896 Life of William Morris, British designer, craftsman, and writer.

1838–1914 Life of John Muir, Scottish-born American naturalist.

1872 Yellowstone becomes the United States' and world's first national park.

1879 Royal National Park opens near Sydney, Australia, as world's second national park.

1885 Banff National Park opens in Alberta, Canada, as first Canadian national park.

1890 Yosemite Valley, in California, becomes a national park.

1892 The Sierra Club is founded in California.

1908 US National Conservation Commission is appointed by President Theodore Roosevelt.

1912–2009 Life of Arne Naess, Norwegian philosopher and eco-warrior.

1916 US National Park Service is set up.

1925 Volcanoes National Park, Rwanda, is established.

1927 Great Mississippi Flood leads to building of dams and levees.

1951 The Peak District becomes the first national park in Britain.

1952 London smog kills 4,000 and leads to laws promoting clean air.

1962 Publication of *Silent Spring* (against pesticide use) by Rachel Carson (1907–1964).

1969 Friends of the Earth is founded by David Brower (1912–2000).

1970 First Earth Day is held on 22 April.

1971 Greenpeace is founded.

1972 United Nations Environment Programme (UNEP) is founded.
Manuel Antonio National Park, Costa Rica, is set up.
First World Environment Day is held on 5 June.

1979 Publication of James Lovelock's *Gaia: A New Look at Life on Earth*.

1983 West German Green Party wins seats in government.

1986 Major nuclear power-plant accident occurs at Chernobyl, Ukraine.

1988 Intergovernmental Panel on Climate Change (IPCC) is established.

1989 *Exxon Valdez* tanker spills huge amounts of oil off Alaska.

1990 First IPCC report on climate change is published.

1992 UN Conference on Environment and Development is held in Rio de
Janeiro, Brazil.

1993 Forest Stewardship Council is established.

1994 European Environment Agency starts work in Copenhagen, Denmark.

1994–2014 Three Gorges hydroelectric project is built in China.

1996 UN Convention to Combat Desertification (UNCCD) comes into force.
Eight countries form the Arctic Council.

1999 European Union Landfill Directive comes into force.

2000 European Landscape Convention comes into force.

2001 Global Greens worldwide network is formed.

2005 Kyoto Protocol, the international treaty on global warming, comes
into force, committing countries to reduction targets for greenhouse
gas emissions.

2007 Former US Vice President Al Gore and the IPCC jointly win the
Nobel Peace Prize for their work to counteract man-made climate change.
Fourth IPCC report on climate change is published.

2010 UN climate conference takes place in Cancún, Mexico.

2011 Major nuclear power-plant accident occurs at Fukushima, Japan.
Serious flooding of the Mississippi River causes opening of spillways.

2014 Fifth IPCC report on climate change is expected to be published.

GLOSSARY

afforestation planting trees to turn land into forest

algae group of simple plant-like organisms that includes seaweed

biodegradable (of substances) that will decay and break down naturally over a period of time

biodiversity wide variety of living things

biofuel fuel produced from plants such as maize, soya beans, or sugar cane

biomass organic matter (such as plants) used as a source of energy

carbon capture and storage (CCS) process of removing carbon dioxide from coal and storing it deep underground

carbon emissions producing and giving off carbon dioxide as a waste gas

certify state that something has reached a certain standard (such as forests being properly managed)

contaminated spoiled by harmful substances; polluted

deforestation the cutting down of trees to clear an area of forest

degrade (land) lose quality, wear away, and become barren

desalination the process of removing salt from seawater

desertification the process of fertile land turning into desert

developer person or company that buys land in order to build on it

ecosystem group of living things that depend on each other and their environment

ecotourist tourist who visits natural, unspoiled environments and tries to avoid damaging these areas

environmental impact assessment statement presented to governmental authorities by developers that describe the environmental impact that a proposed development would have, and how it could be avoided

estuary where the tide from the sea and the river meet

European Union (EU) an association of 27 European countries that allows them to act as a common market for trade

geologist scientist who studies the structure of the Earth

geothermal produced by Earth's natural underground heat

geyser hot spring where boiling water and steam shoot up high in the air

global warming rising temperatures worldwide, caused by an increase of gases in the atmosphere that trap the Sun's heat

greenhouse gas gas that stores heat in the atmosphere. Carbon dioxide and methane are examples of greenhouse gases.

greenwashing term coined by environmentalists to describe what a business or practice does when it falsely claims to be sensitive to the environment

hydroelectric plant water-powered station that generates electricity

hypothesis proposed explanation that leads to further investigation

Industrial Revolution period when Britain and other countries changed from agricultural to industrial nations, with many factories, in the 18th and 19th centuries

levee embankment built to prevent flooding

methane gas that is the main element in natural gas and is given off by rotting plants and manure

Middle Ages period of European history from about the 12th to 15th centuries

opencast mine mine in which ore is extracted at the surface rather than under ground

philosopher person who studies the nature of knowledge; a great thinker

reforestation the replanting of trees to turn land back into forest

rotate grow crops alternately (or one after another) on a piece of land

salt marsh coastal grassland that is regularly flooded with seawater

ship elevator huge machine that lifts ships from one level of water to another

Soviet bloc group of countries that were linked to the former Soviet Union (or USSR, 1922–1991). The largest Soviet republic was Russia.

spit deposited landform found off coasts

sustainable does not use up too many natural resources or pollute the environment

tailings waste left after ore has been extracted from rock

terrace flat area made on a hillside

tungsten hard, strong, grey metal used in old-fashioned light bulbs

UNESCO World Heritage Site place listed by the United Nations Educational, Scientific, and Cultural Organization as being specially important

United Nations (UN) worldwide organization that promotes international peace, security, and cooperation

wave farm collection of machines at sea or on the coast that use the power of waves to generate electricity

wildlife corridor strip of land that acts as a safe passage for wild animals between two habitats

FIND OUT MORE

For further information, you could look at interesting books, films, and websites about green issues and the environment.

Books

The Environment (From Fail to Win), Mary Colson (Raintree, 2010)
Global Warming (What If We Do Nothing?), Neil Morris (Watts, 2007)
Sustaining Our Natural Resources (The Environment Challenge),
  Jen Green (Raintree, 2011)
What's the Point of Being Green?, Jacqui Bailey (Watts, 2010)

Films/DVDs

An Inconvenient Truth (Paramount, 2006), see page 14.
Waste Land by Lucy Walker (Entertainment One, 2011), an Oscar-nominated
  documentary about turning landfill waste into art.
Yellowstone (BBC, 2009), all about the world's first national park.

Websites

Friends of the Earth International, "the world's largest grassroots environmental network" (with links to national websites): **www.foei.org**

Greenpeace International, "an independent global campaigning organization" (with links to national websites): **www.greenpeace.org**

Rainforest Action Network, "campaigns for the forests … through education, grassroots organizing, and non-violent direct action": **www.ran.org**

United Nations Environmental Programme (UNEP) includes topics such as ecosystem management and environmental governance: **www.unep.org**

United States Environmental Protection Agency, with a link to a list of topics, such as landfills, and landscape ecology: **www.epa.gov**

Topics to investigate

There are many different topics related to environmentalism and the landscape. Here are some more research ideas.

Climate change

The International Energy Agency (www.iea.org) says that global carbon dioxide emissions in 2010 were the highest ever recorded. Yet still there are climate change sceptics, people who believe that environmentalists are exaggerating the problems of the enhanced greenhouse effect and global warming. Use a search engine to research climate change and the latest figures. What effects will this have on the landscape?

Connecting "sensitive landscapes"

The European Green Belt initiative (www.europeangreenbelt.org) aims to create an ecological network running from the Barents Sea to the Black Sea. It will connect national parks and nature reserves, spanning 23 countries, stretching for about 8,500 kilometres (5,300 miles), and crossing "impressive and sensitive landscapes". Is this a good green development?

Professional environmentalism

Are you interested in working for the environment? You will find some ideas on pages 26–29, and there are many more job opportunities. One is the field of landscape architecture (the design of sustainable landscape schemes). Put the phrase into a search engine and see what the job involves. Or research other topics, such as "sustainable development".

Do environmentalists always get it right?

Scientists, governments, and environmentalists are learning all the time, sometimes from their own mistakes. For instance, many environmentalists were pleased when the European Union decided that biofuels should make up 10 per cent of fuel sales for transport by 2020. But a survey by the Institute for European Environment Policy showed that this decision would be bad for the environment. The increase in farmland needed to grow the biofuel plants would mean cutting down trees and releasing more carbon dioxide into the atmosphere. So perhaps the EU got it wrong, because the benefits of using biofuels are outweighed by the environmental disadvantages. You could research some other examples of this.

INDEX